GRANDMA,
I WANT TO BE
THE BOSS

WRITTEN BY MICHELE TOWERY

WestBow Press books may be ordered through booksellers or by contacting:

WestBow Press
A Division of Thomas Nelson & Zondervan
1663 Liberty Drive
Bloomington, IN 47403
www.westbowpress.com
1 (866) 928-1240

ISBN: 978-1-9736-0706-9 (sc)
ISBN: 978-1-9736-0705-2 (e)

Library of Congress Control Number: 2017915724

Print information available on the last page.

WestBow Press rev. date: 10/25/2017

WESTBOW
PRESS®
A DIVISION OF THOMAS NELSON
& ZONDERVAN

GRANDMA,
I WANT TO BE
THE BOSS

My name is Daniel and I love my grandma. I wish I could go to her house every day because she is so much fun! We arrive at her house in our big red car and I wave to her. I am very excited.

When Grandma and I are inside, I ask, "Can we cook, go to the lake and play with blocks?"

"Of course I think we can do all those things," replies Grandma.

"Grandma, there are also two things I don't want.
I don't want is to clean up and I don't want to sleep.

Also, I want to be the
boss of everything.
I want to be the king
of bosses!"

3

Grandma says, "I don't think it would be good for you to be the boss of everything, but how about we cook like you want?"

"Can we make pancakes?"

"Of course!"

I put the milk, flour and butter into the bowl. I need to add eggs.

Grandma says, "Let me crack the eggs."

4

I want to be the boss, so I reach for the eggs and crack one anyway. It slides onto the floor.

I say, "I'm the boss and I don't want to clean up the egg."

"We can't finish the pancakes until the mess is cleaned up. Would you like me to help you?"

"Okay."

6

When we are done making the pancakes, I spread butter and syrup. I taste the butter and syrup with my fingers, Yum, yum!

Next, we walk down a long path to a shallow lake. I hold Grandma's hand. I love holding her hand because I love her soooooo much!

Grandma gives me special food for the ducks and says, "Stay on the grass. Don't go near the edge. If you fall into the water, I don't have a towel or dry clothes here."

9

The ducks are hungry and I feed them. After this, I say to myself that I'm the boss and that I can go as close to the edge as I want. Then, when I feed the ducks from the edge, I fall into the water.

Now we have to go home and get a towel and dry clothes!" says Grandma.

So I'm wet and cold, and now I can't finish feeding the ducks like I want.

I cry.

12

Later, when I finish getting my dry clothes on, we play with blocks. We build towers and a whole city. I knock them down and laugh. Grandma laughs too.

Pretty soon she says, "We need to be done now, so let's clean up."

"I don't want to clean up, I want to be the boss of clean up!"

"It's time to clean up, Daniel, and I will help you."

14

"I don't want to clean up.
I don't want to clean up!"

I run away fast.

15

I hide in the closet next to the vacuum. It's very quiet in here. I put one finger to my lips.

I say quietly to the vacuum, "Shusssssh."

I don't hear my grandma. I worry because it has been a long time that she hasn't found me.

I peek out of the closet and don't see Grandma. I look everywhere in the house for her. Tears wet my face, I cry. It seems like my grandma has disappeared. I wipe the tears off with my sleeve and look in Grandma's big bedroom.

When I don't find her there, I cry loudly with tears wetting my clothes.

Next, I run outside to find her.

When I find her, I say, "I'm sorry Grandma, you can be the boss of clean up."

We hug.

When we walk back into the house, Grandma says, "It's naptime Daniel."

"I'm the boss of naps and I won't sleep!"

"Just lie down and rest, my sweety—pie, Daniel. You can be the boss of resting or sleeping."

I walk to Grandma's bedroom. I climb up onto her tall bed using a stepstool.

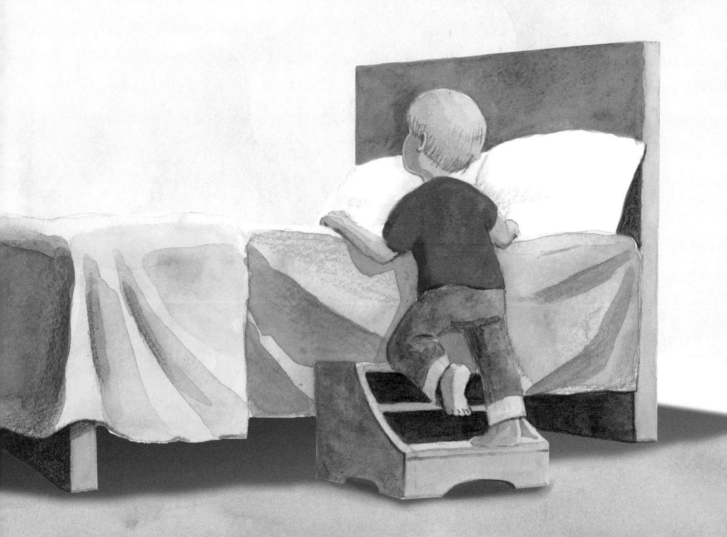

I lie down and think to myself. It seems that I'm not very good at choosing when to be the boss: When I crack the egg, anyway, I have to clean up. When I get too close to the edge of the lake, anyway, I fall into the water. Because of getting wet and cold I can't finish feeding the ducks. When I run away Grandma seems missing. Maybe Grandma can be the boss sometimes.

Pretty soon, it's time to go home
and I don't want to, so I run behind
the couch.

Grandma finds me and says, "You can come back real soon, Daniel."

"Okay Grandma, and I will share being boss with you."

"That sounds good to me."

We hug.

I say, "I love you
Grandma. Bye,
bye my grandma."